D1558034

MOVIEMAKERS' FILM CLUB

Be a FILM DIRECTOR

Direct with CONFIDENCE

by
Alix Wood

PowerKiDS press

New York

Published in 2018 by Rosen Publishing
29 East 21st Street, New York, NY 10010

CATALOGING-IN-PUBLICATION DATA

Names: Wood, Alix.
Title: Be a film director: direct with confidence / Alix Wood.
Description: New York : PowerKids Press, 2018. | Series: Moviemakers' film club | Includes index.
Identifiers: LCCN ISBN 9781538323724 (pbk.) | ISBN 9781538322765 (library bound) | ISBN 9781538323731 (6 pack)
Subjects: LCSH: Motion pictures--Production and direction--Juvenile literature.
Classification: LCC PN1994.5 W64 2018 | DDC 791.43023--dc23

Produced for Rosen Publishing by Alix Wood Books
Designed by Alix Wood
Editor: Eloise Macgregor
Editor for Rosen: Kerri O'Donnell
Series consultant: Cameron Browne

Photo credits: Cover, 1, 4, 6, 7, 8, 10, 11 top, 12, 13, 14, 15, 16, 17, 19, 21, 24, 26, 28, 29 © Adobe Stock Images; 11 bottom © Shutterstock; 22 © Alix Wood; 23 © Cameron Browne, 25 © DoD; 27 © Denis Makarenko/Dreamstime

Printed in the United States of America
CPSIA compliance information: Batch # BW18PK: For further information contact Rosen Publishing, New York, New York at 1-800-542-2595.

CONTENTS

INTRODUCING THE DIRECTOR!

The lighting team has a problem with making the sunset look realistic. You talk through some of their ideas. Then the accountant calls. She's worried about the movie's **budget**. You give her some ideas on how you might cut your spending. You get back to the scene you are filming. The actor's emotion just isn't quite right – how can you help fix it?

A director needs to be comfortable being in charge. They control every part of the movie from beginning to end. Before filming even starts, they approve the **script**, the **locations**, and help choose the right actors to play the parts. On set, the director works with the actors, lighting, camera, and sound departments to make sure that all of the elements come together. After filming stops, the director will watch over the **editing**, too.

A director has to be confident leading a team of people. They need to motivate and inspire everyone to produce the best possible movie.

Cell Phone Movie School

Want to start thinking like a director? Watch as many films as you can. Choose some scenes that you liked the best and watch them over and over. Analyze what it was about them that worked for you. See if you can spot any mistakes, either in the acting, or the filming, or the story. Start to develop a critical eye.

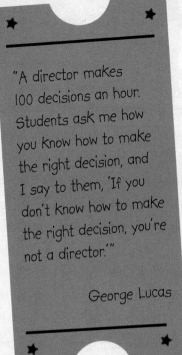

"A director makes 100 decisions an hour. Students ask me how you know how to make the right decision, and I say to them, 'If you don't know how to make the right decision, you're not a director.'"

George Lucas

A director needs to...

- love making films
- be a confident leader
- be happy making decisions
- be creative
- be able to imagine a story in moving pictures
- create good relationships with people they work with
- be a good communicator
- inspire and motivate people
- trust other people to carry out their wishes
- understand the technical and creative parts of filmmaking
- be happy working long hours
- pay attention to detail
- be calm under pressure
- be determined

WORKING TOGETHER

People skills are very important when you are a director. Even though the director is in charge of filming, they have a boss in charge of them, too. Directors work for the **movie studio**, and the movie's **producer**. Directors have to be able to deal with people at all levels and be able to persuade those above or below them what will be best for the movie.

Communicate The Vision

A director should have a vision in their head of how the final movie will look. They then must explain that vision to everyone else. In any one day, a movie director might work with actors, makeup artists, the director of photography, scriptwriters, the sound designer, and the lighting or visual effects experts.

A director needs to trust their team. A good director will always ask their crew's advice on the best way to achieve their vision.

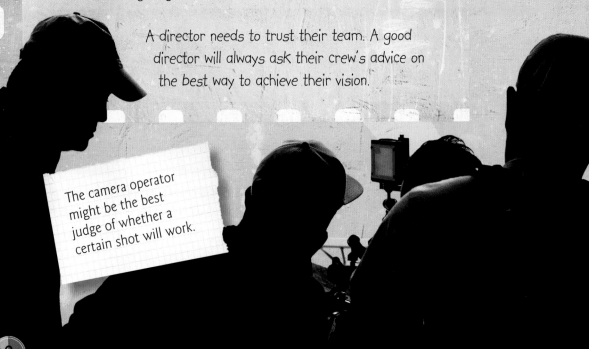

The camera operator might be the best judge of whether a certain shot will work.

When a director wins an award, they will almost always thank their team in their speech!

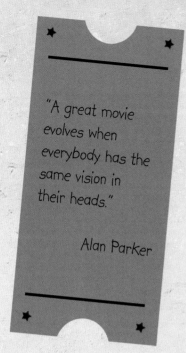

"A great movie evolves when everybody has the same vision in their heads."

Alan Parker

Don't expect too much praise. Usually when a movie does well, the actors get most of the credit. However, when a movie goes badly, the director will usually get the blame!

Cell Phone Movie School

How good are your people skills? As a director you will need to be excellent at the art of keeping people happy. Are you persuasive? Are you **diplomatic**? Personal skills are as important as artistic or technical ability. Studio bosses hire directors they like to work with. In the same way, directors often hire the same team to work with them on several movies. If you are unpleasant to work with, the best crews may look elsewhere for their next movie. Be polite and respectful. Listen carefully to people's concerns. You don't have to agree with them, but everyone wants to be listened to.

FINDING A SCRIPT

Big Hollywood directors are given piles of great scripts to choose from for their next movie. Starting out, you may not be so lucky! So, how do you get a great story? If you have some writing talent you could write your own script. Perhaps you have a friend with an interesting idea for a movie who would be good at screenwriting?

Cell Phone Movie School

To help decide whether your script is good enough, ask yourself these questions:

- Does the story make sense?
- Is there an event that will hook in the audience?
- Is the plot interesting?
- Are there good, strong characters?
- Does the story interest you?

As director, you will have to love and believe in your story. You will be putting your own money, time, sweat, and tears into making that movie.

A good script will hook you in on the first few pages, so you want to read more.

The Hero's Journey

Does your script follow a hero's journey? Writer Joseph Campbell noticed that good stories from all around the world often follow a basic pattern, known as "the hero's journey." The main character leaves their everyday life to go on an adventure, where they win a victory, and then return home changed.

When you read your script, think about how you would bring each scene to life on film. What camera angles would you use? What sound effects would you need? Would you need special lighting?

Read other people's scripts to learn the correct way to write them. The right **format** makes the script easier to direct.

Pages are numbered.

2.

FADE IN:

They say where the action takes place. EXT. means exterior, INT. means interior.

EXT. ALEX'S HOUSE - DAY

A cab drives slowly past.

There may be a brief description of the scene.

ALEX runs out of the front door and waves. The cab stops, and reverses.

                    CAB DRIVER
          You Alex?

Character names are usually written in capital letters.

Stage directions are written in brackets.

                    ALEX
               (impatient)
          Yes, yes. Where have you been?

CAB DRIVER shrugs

                    ALEX (CONT'D)
          Help get this pig in the
          trunk. Don't worry, it's dead.

9

STORYBOARDS

Once you have chosen your script, create a storyboard. A storyboard is a hand-drawn version of your movie. It breaks the movie down, bit by bit, into separate shots, to help plan how you will film the action. A storyboard also allows you to check your ideas work, before you get on set.

You don't have to be amazing at drawing. You can draw a storyboard using simple stick figures. Try to include the foreground, mid-ground, and background when you have them in shot. This helps to give your scene its setting and clearly show any camera angles that you might want to use.

background

mid-ground

foreground

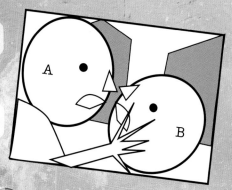

If you have several characters in your drawing, an easy way to see who is who is to label each of them, A, B, C, and so on.

Cell Phone Movie School

There are a few different ways to create a storyboard. You can buy special storyboard pads from art stores and draw them by hand. Some people draw each shot on sticky notes and stick them to a board, instead. This allows you to move the order of the shots around easily. Some **apps** and **software** let you create storyboards on your phone or computer. See if any of your software has a storyboard feature.

Shot 1 Close-up	BUS Picture on phone of Tom and Hayley

Shot 2 Pull back	BUS See Tom's hand holding phone

Shot 3 Long shot	BUS Tom stands, holding phone

Storyboards briefly describe each shot.

If you really don't trust your drawing skills, you could take photographs instead. Use friends to stand in for the actors and snapshots for your storyboard.

FINANCING A MOVIE

Now that you have your storyboard ready, you can go and sell your idea. Movies can be very expensive to make. Studios won't want to pay for a movie unless they think it will be a big success. It's time to start selling your idea.

Established directors will contact the movie studios and set up meetings to try to sell their idea. When you first start out, no studio will want to meet with you. It takes many years and plenty of luck to make it as a big-time director. Most young filmmakers will have to raise the money themselves. That doesn't always mean setting up a lemonade stand in front of your house, but it might!

LEMONADE
15¢

Work out a budget for your movie. Even if all your actors and crew are friends working for free, you may still have other costs. Do you need to buy any filming equipment or **props**, or pay for transportation to your locations? Time to start saving your allowance!

Many independent young filmmakers raise their money using websites such as Kickstarter. These sites ask for money to fund a project, with the promise of something in return. Movie projects often promise a credit in the movie titles, or a ticket to the premier!

B 002536 - 1

Cell Phone Movie School

You can use social media to promote your movie. Always check with an adult before you do this, though. You do not want to give personal information to strangers. Make a page or blog about your movie and post about its progress. Create posters and **teasers** to put on your blog. Hopefully, friends will start to follow you and get excited about your project.

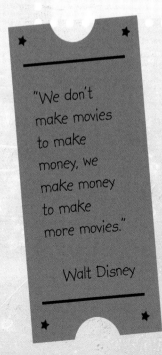

"We don't make movies to make money, we make money to make more movies."

Walt Disney

Careful Planning Saves Money

Make sure that you keep track of your budget. If you plan your movie carefully, you can help keep the costs down. Try creating a story that only uses one or two locations. That way, any travel costs will be lower. Use the cheapest equipment that you can. Remember that the story is the most important thing. What equipment you used to film your story doesn't really matter.

CHOOSING THE RIGHT ACTORS

MOVIE AUDITION →

Actors will make or break a movie. Directors are usually involved with **casting** the main parts, often with the help of a casting director. The casting director will normally cast the smaller roles by themselves.

Finding Actors

Big-budget movies use **agents** to find actors for their movie casting sessions. Smaller budget movies may post advertisements on websites that actors use, briefly explaining the project and inviting actors to come for casting.

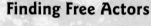

Finding Free Actors

For a no-budget movie, you need to be more inventive to get your great actors! Try these tips.

- Pin a flyer on your school bulletin board.
- Contact local drama groups.
- Ask friends to recommend people to you.

Hopefully, you'll get a line of actors waiting to be in your movie!

Cell Phone Movie School

Ask your actors to do an **audition**. Get someone else to help you, and give them a copy of the script. They can help the actor with their lines if they stumble. Then you will be able to concentrate on watching the actor's performance. It is a good idea to record their auditions, to help you remember what each actor was like.

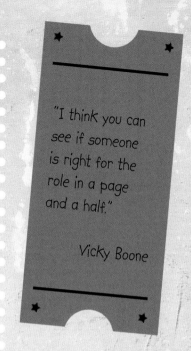

"I think you can see if someone is right for the role in a page and a half."

Vicky Boone

Remember that auditions can be scary. You want to make your actors feel comfortable. If someone feels comfortable they are more likely to give a good performance. Hold your auditions in a quiet room, with a separate waiting area. Be friendly, and explain a little about the movie. Allow enough time to get to know each actor.

After their audition, thank each actor for their time and compliment them on the parts they did well. Tell them when you will let them know if they have a part. Contact everyone, even if you don't want them in the movie. It is hard to give bad news, but it is better for the actor to know than to be left waiting.

FINDING LOCATIONS

On a big film production, a location manager will usually be in charge of finding locations. First, they might look through their files to see if they have anything suitable. If they can't find a good location there, they'll widen their search. Location managers will usually involve the director before making a final decision.

Location Checklist

- Is the location essential? Each new location adds cost!
- Is the location right for the movie?
- Will it be easy to travel to?
- Are there enough facilities for everyone?
- Is there electricity?
- Is there available light?
- What is the weather usually like?
- Do we need permission to film there? Can we get it?

"All these directors who do different locations forget that one room can be shot from a million different angles."

Michael Pitt

Photograph your locations when you are scouting, so you can remember them. At outdoor locations, take shots from all angles. Bring a compass so you can see which direction the sun rises and sets.

Cell Phone Movie School

Make your location work for you. This abandoned building (right) allows the camera operators to get some great aerial shots without having to use expensive equipment. Make sure you stay safe, though. Ask an adult to help you choose your location, and help check that you have permission to film there. Being on property without permission is a crime, so don't risk it.

Make sure your sound and camera crew check your location for annoying noises, or poor light.

MAKING A SHOT LIST

Before you start shooting your movie, you may want to create a shot list. A shot list is a numbered list of every shot, in order, for the whole movie. A director can't be everywhere at once. A shot list gives all the information the crew should need. They can check the list for answers to any questions without bothering the director.

Directors usually use their storyboard to help them make their shot list. A shot list has a lot more technical information than a storyboard, though.

These terms are explained on page 19

What Goes On a Shot List

A director will usually put the following information on a shot list.

- The shot number
- The type of shot
- The size of the shot
- If the camera needs to move
- The angle of the camera
- The location
- A brief description of the action in the shot
- If any characters are in the shot
- If any props are needed
- How long the shot will last

Shot No	Type	Size	Movement	Angle	Location	Action	Actors	Props	Length
1	EST	WS	**Pan**	N	EXT. Farm	Car arrives	Tom		4 secs
2	ONE SHOT	WS		N	EXT. Farm	Tom exits car	Tom	Case	2 secs
3	ONE SHOT	CU		N	EXT. Farm	Looks worried	Tom	Case	2 secs
4	ONE SHOT	LS	Pan	N	EXT. Farm	Tom slowly walks up steps	Tom	Case	3 secs
5	TWO SHOT	OTS		Low	EXT. Farm	Alex opens door	Tom Alex	Case	2 secs

Types of Shot

Establishing shot (EST) a shot that shows the setting.

Interior (INT) indoor shot.

Exterior (EXT) outside shot.

Two shot (TWO SHOT) shows two characters in a frame.

Single shot (or one shot) (ONE SHOT) shows a single character in a frame.

Point of view (POV) shot as if seen from a character's eyes.

Over the shoulder (OTS) taken from over the shoulder of one character toward another.

Wide shot (WS) a view showing scenery.

Medium, or **mid shot** (MS) shows a character to the waist.

Close-up (CU) a close-up showing head and shoulders.

Extreme close-up (XCU) a close-up of a section of the face.

Establishing shot

Point of view   Extreme close-up

Cell Phone Movie School

A movie is not usually filmed in the order a script or shot list is written. Another list, known as the shooting schedule, shows the order of each day's shoot. The shots are grouped to catch the same lighting, or to film all the shots using a particular camera setup at once.

CAMERA MOVES

A director's shot list will say if the camera has to move. It is important for the crew to know in advance. They may have to set up special equipment, or get a **grip** to help push the camera along.

Different Camera Moves

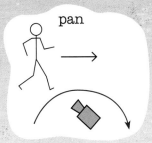

pan

Pan	The camera stays still, but pivots side to side.
Tilt	The camera stays still but pivots up and down.
Pedestal	The camera moves up and down without tilting.
Dolly	The camera moves forward or backward, sometimes on a wheeled platform on a track.
Truck	The same as dollying, only the camera moves from left to right.
Arc	A dolly or truck with a curve in the track.
Handheld	The camera is held by the operator.
Steadicam	The camera operator wears a special rig that stabilizes the camera as they follow the action.
Crane	A shot that starts very high and moves lower or vice versa.

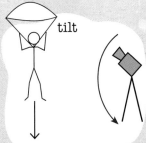

tilt

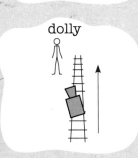

dolly

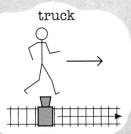

truck

Camera angles

Directors use different camera angles to help tell their story. Camera angles can change our attitude toward an object or character. Eye level is the most normal angle, with the camera acting like a person watching the scene. Shooting from a high angle can make the subject seem weak and powerless. A low camera angle, looking up at a character, makes them appear powerful.

low-angle shot

A crane can get a great establishing shot. A director might start this shot zoomed in on one umbrella, and then gradually pull back to show the setting.

Cell Phone Movie School

Try filming a friend or toy from different angles using a smartphone. See what different emotions you can bring to each shot. Try taking shots from below, or above. Try a pedestal shot – move the camera slowly up from the toes to the head. A slow pedestal shot can make something seem very tall.

THE REHEARSAL

Once all the planning stages are done, it's time for action! Before the camera rolls, the director organizes the rehearsal. It is important to run through each shot with the actors and the crew. The director works closely with the 1st Assistant Director, who controls the set.

Actors need to know where they will be during filming. If they have to move, they need to know where to, when, and how they move. Working out an actor's movements is known as **blocking**. It is important that the camera, sound, and lighting department are involved in any discussion about blocking. The actor's movement will affect where the crew can set up their equipment, and what equipment they will need.

Helpful Diagrams

Another tool directors can use to plan movement is the **overhead**. An overhead is a bird's-eye view diagram of every shot. Characters are drawn as circles with triangle noses or stripes showing the direction they are facing. Numbered points with arrows between them show the character movement. Cameras are "V" shapes, and may also have arrows showing movement.

A rehearsal is essential for everyone on set. A busy location can get quite chaotic. Everyone needs to know what to do once the cameras start rolling.

Cell Phone Movie School

Practice the script with your actors before the set rehearsal. This will help make sure they know their lines and are happy with what they need to say. Once the actors feel comfortable with the words, they can start worrying about moving around, and adding emotions. It's a good idea to roughly film the rehearsal and watch it before the actual filming, to see if you can help improve the scene.

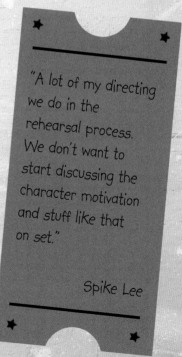

"A lot of my directing we do in the rehearsal process. We don't want to start discussing the character motivation and stuff like that on set."

Spike Lee

MOTIVATING ACTORS

One of the main things a director has to do is motivate actors to give their best performance. It can be difficult being a movie actor. Often, scenes are filmed out of order. An actor may need help with what their character is feeling during the action you are filming that day. To be able to help them, a director needs to know the script inside out.

An actor and director thinking through their next scene.

To understand the problems an actor faces, it is a good idea for a director to learn to act. Walking in an actor's shoes may help a director understand the motivation needed for a scene.

Cell Phone Movie School

A character should say a line differently if they are upset, or angry, or proud. If you are not happy with how the actor says a line, try to give precise instructions. Don't say "Try it again," say "Try it again a little angrier." Make sure you praise everything that goes right. It will help encourage your actors and let them know when they are on the right track.

Movie extras often have no acting experience at all. Here, director Michael Bay is taking time to explain what he wants from some military movie extras on the set of *Transformers*.

"I've always said the one advantage an actor has of converting to a director is that he's been in front of the camera."
Clint Eastwood

DIRECTING THE EDIT

Even after the film has been shot and all the actors have moved on to their next project, the director will still be working on the movie. Called post-production, this final stage of moviemaking is very important.

The director will work with the editor, **visual effects** team, sound designer, and composer to put the finishing touches to the movie. Days of filming are carefully edited to create the best possible version of the story. The music and sound effects are added to the soundtrack. Actors' lines may have to be re-recorded to be sure they are the best possible quality.

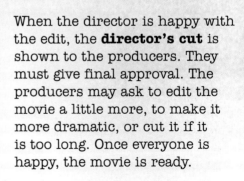

When the director is happy with the edit, the **director's cut** is shown to the producers. They must give final approval. The producers may ask to edit the movie a little more, to make it more dramatic, or cut it if it is too long. Once everyone is happy, the movie is ready.

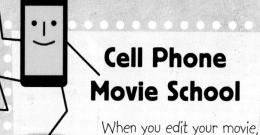

Cell Phone Movie School

When you edit your movie, you will want to make sure the story keeps your audience gripped. Cut out any boring bits. You may find a lot of your footage has nothing really happening in it. You may have a shot of a door which starts to open. Did you need the footage of the closed door? If the closed door helps build suspense, keep it in. If it doesn't, cut it out.

Letting Go

You can shorten a film by around ten percent through trimming bits from your scenes. If your movie needs to be even shorter, whole scenes may have to be cut. This can be hard for a director to do, as they have put so much work into them. That is why it helps to have an editor who is not so involved in the filming to decide what works and what doesn't.

Once your movie is finished, it's time to get your best clothes on and take a walk down the red carpet for your movie premiere!

Director Sean Penn on the red carpet, attending a movie premiere with his children.

27

MAKING YOUR NAME

The best way to get experience as a director is to get a group of friends together and start making movies. Shoot as much film as you can to practice your skills. Once you have a selection of work that you are proud of, make a **showreel**.

Cell Phone Movie School

A showreel is a short collection of a person's movie "best bits." A director's showreel should focus on directing skills, such as the performance that they got out of their actors. When you make your showreel, try to link clips to tell a story. Add variety with a mix of happy, sad, funny, and action scenes. If you add a few seconds of shorter clips, choose music that works with them all. Don't make every cut line up with the beat, though, or it becomes too predictable. Add some sound effects, too, as a professional finishing touch.

"Pick up a camera. Shoot something. No matter how small, no matter how cheesy, no matter whether your friends and your sister star in it...Now you're a director. Everything after that you're just negotiating your budget and your fee."

James Cameron

Getting Known

Once you have your showreel ready, you need to start **networking**. Meeting people in the movie industry is the best way to get someone to watch your reel. If you can, go to local film festivals, conventions, and movie premieres.

Offering to help other moviemakers or drama groups for free is a good way of getting known and making friends, too. Ask your drama teacher if they would let you film your school play.

If you have any friends in a band, you could offer to direct a music video for them.

Movie Competitions and Festivals

One way to get your film noticed by a bigger audience is to enter it in a film competition. Look for competitions with school categories, which might be free to enter. Many competitions ask for money. This is because they are sent so many movies, the money pays for the time it takes the judges to watch them.

Film festivals will often help young filmmakers by holding workshops and lectures. See if there are any festivals in your area that you could attend. Then have fun making movies!

GLOSSARY

agents People who find jobs for actors.

apps Applications.

audition A short performance to test the talents of a musician, singer, dancer, or actor.

blocking Working out an actor's movements in a scene.

budget The amount of money available for some purpose.

casting Assigning parts to actors.

close-ups Film images taken at close range and showing the subject on a large scale.

crane A machine with a swinging arm for lifting and carrying heavy weights.

diplomatic Tactful.

director's cut A version of a film that reflects the director's original intentions.

dolly A small platform on wheels used for holding heavy objects.

editing Arranging, revising, and preparing a movie for final production.

establishing shot Usually the first shot of a new scene, to show where the action is taking place.

format The general organization or arrangement of something.

grips Member of the camera crew who sets up, moves, builds, and maintains equipment.

handheld A camera that is held by the operator.

locations Places away from a studio where a movie is shot.

movie studio A place where motion pictures are made.

networking Interact with others to exchange information and develop professional or social contacts.

overhead A bird's-eye-view diagram of a camera shot.

over the shoulder A shot taken from over the shoulder of one character toward another.

pan Moving the camera horizontally so that it sweeps around the scene.

pedestal shot Moving the camera up or down without changing its vertical or horizontal axis.

point of view Footage that is shot as if seen from a character's eyes.

producer A person who supervises or finances a movie.

props Objects used in a movie.

script The written text of a play or movie.

showreel A short videotape of examples of an actor's or director's work for showing to potential employers.

software The programs and other operating information used by a computer.

stage directions Instructions indicating the movement, position, or tone of an actor, or the sound effects and lighting.

steadicam A lightweight mounting for a film camera which keeps it steady for filming when handheld or moving.

teasers An advertising or promotional device intended to arouse interest.

tilt Where the camera stays in a fixed position but rotates up and down in a vertical plane.

visual effects A special effect that is added to a film or video in post-production.

FOR MORE INFORMATION

Books

O'Neill, Joseph. *Movie Director (21st Century Skills Library: Cool Careers)*, North Mankato, MN: Cherry Lake Publishing, 2013.

Stoller, Bryan Michael. *Smartphone Movie Maker*. Somerville, MA: Candlewick, 2017.

Websites

Due to the changing nature of Internet links, PowerKids Press has developed an online list of websites related to the subject of this book. This site is updated regularly. Please use this link to access the list:

www.powerkidslinks.com/mm/director

INDEX